NOT-FOR-PARENTS

SOUTH AMERICA
Everything you ever wanted to know

Margaret Hynes

C015850753

CONTENTS

LET'S START AT THE BEGINNING...

NOT-FOR-PARENTS

THIS IS NOT A GUIDEBOOK. And it is definitely Not-for-Parents.

IT IS THE REAL INSIDE STORY about one of the world's most colourful continents – South America. In this book you'll hear fascinating tales about wrestling ladies and man-eating fish, lost cities, intrepid explorers and **remarkable survivals**.

Check out cool stories about the real **Robinson Crusoe**, a navy without an ocean, rivers that shimmer with colours and floating islands. You'll find dirty dancing, **fowl play**, daring prison escapes and **history** galore.

This book shows you a **SOUTH AMERICA** your parents probably don't even know about.

WHAT'S IN A NAME?

Most of the country names in South America make a lot of sense when you know the history and geography of the continent. Colombia was named after Christopher Columbus, one of the first European explorers to set foot on the continent. Guyana has lots of rivers, and its name means 'land of many waters' in the native Amerindian language. Its position on the Equator gives Ecuador its name. But some names aren't so appropriate.

Fool's silver

In the early 16th century, Spanish adventurers called conquistadores travelled to the northeastern part of what is now Argentina, having heard there were mountains of silver there. They named the region La Argentina, which comes from the Latin word for silver, 'argentum'. The main river in the area became known as Rio de la Plata, or river of silver. Nice names but no silver has been found there.

VENEZUELA

GUYANA

SURINAME

FRENCH GUIANA

COLOMBIA

ECUADOR

PERU

BRAZIL

BOLIVIA

CHILE

ARGENTINA

URUGUAY

Atlantic Ocean

Pacific Ocean

Not nuts

It was common for 15th- and 16th-century Portuguese people to refer to their colonies by the product they took from it. You may think Brazil was named after Brazil nuts, but it was actually named after brazilwood, a wood that produces a deep-red dye. The colour was hugely popular for clothes in Europe at the time.

Simon Bolívar

I DON'T BOLIVIA!

Simon Bolívar helped much of South America get its independence from the Spanish Empire in the early 1800s, so it's no surprise Bolivia was named after him. The thing is, Bolívar was actually from Venezuela. His home country didn't forget him, though – its official name is the Bolivarian Republic of Venezuela and the name of the currency there is the bolívar.

Venice of the south

In 1499, Italian cartographer Amerigo Vespucci visited the area around Lake Maracaibo in the northwestern part of what is now Venezuela. The stilted houses there reminded him of Venice in Italy, and so he called the region Veneziola, which over time became Venezuela and the name for the whole country.

WANT MORE?

CHILDREN OF THE FOREST

The Yanomami are a forest-dwelling tribe who live in the Amazonian rainforest. About 20,000 Yanomami live in around 250 villages. Village life is centred on a large communal house, called a *yano*. Most children don't go to school. They learn everything they need to know from their elders.

I'M AIMING FOR THE TOP!

Communal living

Some yanos are home to 400 people. A large central area is used for rituals, feasts and games. Each family has its own cooking area with a fire. At night, the family members sleep in hammocks slung near the fire.

Boys will be boys

Boys learn by watching their elders and playing in the jungle. They practise hunting by firing arrows at lizards and birds. They sometimes go on hunting trips with their fathers, or help to make tools. But, until they are about 20 years old, they spend most of the time playing with their friends.

The Yanomami grow crops, as well as gathering and hunting a rich array of foods from the jungle.

I HOPE MY MUM DOESN'T MIND!

Growing up fast!
By the time a Yanomami girl is about nine years old, she is expected to look after the other children in her family. She also has to help her mother with the cooking and other jobs. Most Yanomami girls are married by the age of twelve.

The ear lobes, nose and lips of the boys and girls are often pierced with thin bamboo sticks.

The entire village lives in a single yano.

Annatto pods

TEMPORARY TATTOOS

The Yanomami decorate themselves with body paint for special occasions. They use seeds from the annatto tree to make a red colour. They make black from the fruit from the genipap tree, or a mix of annatto seeds and ashes. The designs are based on forest plants and animals.

WANT MORE?

The Yanomami ☆ www.survivalinternational.org

WHERE DID YOU GET THAT HAT?

You might think that the Panama hat comes from Panama. However, the rather dashing straw-brimmed hat actually comes from Ecuador. It became known as a Panama because in the 19th and 20th centuries, it was shipped to Europe, Asia and the rest of the Americas from Panama.

SO, WHERE DOES IT COME FROM AGAIN?

ECUADOR, OF COURSE!

Genuine article
A panama hat isn't a specific shape. To be called a Panama, the hat must be handwoven with high-quality straw harvested from the *Carludovica palmata* plant, which grows in the foothills of the Andes.

Drying the leaves of the palm

THE FINAL STRAW

Before weaving can begin, the palm fronds must be split open and their fibres stripped out. These are boiled in water for one minute, then hung up to dry. The dry fibres are placed in a box and bleached with smoke. Finally, the fibres are hand split into straw strands fine enough to create an incredibly tight weave.

Hats off to them

A fine Panama hat can take up to three months to make. The hat maker first weaves the top. Then, the weave is turned down over a block to finish the crown shape. Once the brim is woven, the hat is cleaned and bleached, before it is pounded to make it ultra supple. The hat is then trimmed, sized and shaped, before the band is added.

Weaving starts at the top.

The weaver uses his chest to press down on a wooden block to keep the hat in place

Packing a Panama

Well-made Panama hats are very flexible, and one style, known as the 'folder', can be rolled up for travel. Once it is unrolled, it springs back into shape

Panama hit

Panama hats became hugely popular in the mid-19th century, when miners of the Gold Rush picked them up in the Isthmus of Panama on the way to California. Sales were given a further boost when, in 1904, US president Theodore Roosevelt was photographed wearing a Panama on a visit to the construction site of the Panama Canal.

Count on a Montecristi

The most expensive hats are known as Montecristis, after the town where they are made. The hats are so finely woven that they can hold water. When they are rolled up, they are said to be able to pass through a wedding ring.

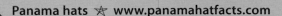

Roosevelt sporting a Panama

WANT MORE?

Panama hats ☆ www.panamahatfacts.com

ANCIENT ARTY FACTS AND FICTION

The Nazca lines are one of the world's greatest mysteries. They are trenches arranged in amazing patterns, which cover a large area of the Nazca Desert in Peru. Created between 200BC and AD500, they continue to baffle archaeologists. While most scientists agree that the people from the Nazca culture created the drawings, no one has proved what they mean. But there have certainly been some very interesting theories.

Spider (left) and tree (below)

Lines in the sand
The parched land and hillsides of the Nazca Desert made the perfect canvas for the ancient artists. By removing a layer of dark stones, the lighter sand beneath was revealed, creating a colour contrast that still stands out today.

Hummingbird

Go figure!
There are hundreds of individual figures. Some look like triangles with the top cut off. Others are more complex and stylized, such as the astronaut and figures of animals, including spiders, hummingbirds, fish, lizards and monkeys. But what do they mean?

The drawings are several kilometres long, and up to 1.1km (0.7mi) wide.

Hummingbird

Monkey

Marked on the calendar
In 1941, Maria Reiche and Paul Kosok discovered that one of the long, straight lines pointed directly at the sunset during the winter solstice on 22 June. When, six months later, they found another line pointing directly at the summer solstice sunset, they came to the conclusion that the lines create a giant astronomical calendar.

WHAT ANIMAL IS THAT?

Maria Reiche and an assistant

Pelican

HEY, WE'VE LEFT OUR MARK!

RAIN RITUALS
Human made mounds of stones littered about the lines contain the remains of shellfish called *Spondylus*. This is a religious symbol of fertility and water in ancient Andean cultures. So, as the region has very little rainfall, the lines and mounds could have been part of a ceremony praying for rain.

The answer is out there
In the 1960s, the Swiss author Erich von Däniken put forward some pretty outlandish theories for the origins of the lines. One of his ideas was that an ancient alien spaceship blew away the rocks as it landed! Another of von Däniken's theories was that the lines formed an elaborate runway system for the alien craft.

Nazca line observation towers are found along the Pan-American Highway, which cuts through the desert.

WANT MORE?

Nazca culture flourished from 100BC to AD800.

THE ANGEL WHO FLEW OVER THE FALLS

The Angel Falls in southeastern Venezuela are named after Jimmie Angel, who became the first person to fly over them in 1933. They were actually given the name after Angel crash-landed on top of Auyantepui, from where the falls cascade, in 1937. It took 11 days for Angel and his three companions to make their way back to civilization, and the falls were named in his honour.

Auyantepui, or Devil's Mountain

Angel Falls spills into Devil's Canyon.

Sticky situation

Looking for gold, Jimmie Angel returned to Auyantepui in his Flamingo monoplane, *El Río Caroní*, in 1937. After landing, the plane's wheels hit marshy ground and sank. The plane then turned on its nose, making take-off impossible.

A TALL STORY?

Angel was searching for metal ore on behalf of a mining company when he first spotted Angel Falls on 18 November 1933. On his return to base, Angel reported that he had seen a 'mile-high waterfall'. Nobody believed him. The falls were later measured at 970m (0.6mi). They might not be a mile high, but they are still the tallest falls in the world.

WOAH! THAT'S GOT TO BE A MILE HIGH!

Jimmie Angel in 1930

Angel's party spent two days trying to salvage the plane.

Angel's escape from the Devil
Angel and his passengers were not harmed during the crash-landing, but they were not out of danger. It took an 11-day trek across difficult terrain and with very little food for them to reach the safety of the nearest settlement at Kamarata.

Fallen angel
El Río Caroní stayed on the mountain until 1970, when it was dismantled and lifted down by Venezuelan military helicopters. The plane was reassembled for display in the city of Maracay's aviation museum.

El Río Caroní

WANT MORE?

Angel Falls ★ www.canyonsworldwide.com/tepui/angelfalls.html

SKIRTS FLY!

A woman flies through the air in a swirl of shiny material and petticoats, and then scrambles to her feet and knocks over her opponent. This, ladies and gentlemen, is 'lucha libre', Bolivia's version of World Wrestling Entertainment (WWE). There may not be spectacular light shows, but you do get Aymara women, known as *cholitas*, dressed up to the nines in traditional costumes, theatrically mauling men and other cholitas.

Sporting traditional dress

The cholitas look like they are dressed for church instead of a wrestling match. Each one wears a shiny skirt over layers of petticoats, with an embroidered shawl and a bowler hat. The women's long hair is braided into plaits.

Hair pulling is encouraged.

COME ON, YOU KNOW I'M THE PRETTIEST!

CROWD PLEASERS

Before the cholitas enter the ring, they twirl and dance until the crowd goes crazy. When they finally get into the ring, both wrestlers try to get the crowd to side with them. Then, off come the bowler hats, and the women launch themselves at each other.

Food fight

The crowd like to get involved, especially to show their displeasure with a baddie or the referee, so it's not unusual to see chicken bones or popcorn flying towards the ring.

She's behind you

In true pantomime form, there are *ruda*, or baddies, and there are *técnica*, or goodies. It soon becomes obvious which is which, and who the crowd will side with. Usually the referee lends a helping hand – to the baddie.

I'LL TEACH YOU TO SAY I'M FAT.

Playing with fire

The women use plenty of well-known wrestling moves, such as half nelsons and headlocks. Then there is plain dirty fighting, with wrestlers thrown out of the ring and chairs thrown. It has been known for the referee to be the victim of a pile driver. Sparks really fly when the cholitas use their most deadly move and set each other alight...

WANT MORE?

Bolivian clothing ★ www.boliviabella.com/bolivian-clothing.html

THE REAL ROBINSON CRUSOE

In 1704, a battle-scarred British ship called *Cinque Ports* anchored off the deserted Juan Fernandez Islands, 600km (373mi) off the coast of Chile. The ship's navigator, Alexander Selkirk, fell out with the captain over the vessel's seaworthiness and demanded to be put ashore. The four years and four months he spent there until he was rescued inspired one of the world's great tales of survival – Daniel Defoe's *Robinson Crusoe*.

SELKIRK WENT ASHORE WITH THESE ITEMS:

Bedding
Musket
Pistol
Gunpowder
Hatchet
Knife

Navigation tools
Pot for boiling food
Tobacco
Cheese
Jam
Flask of rum
Bible

To keep his spirits up, the plucky navigator sang hymns and prayed.

Island life

Elephant seals wailed at night, trees snapped in gales, and rats tore at Selkirk's feet as he slept. In time, Selkirk tamed some wild cats, which became companions – as well as vermin exterminators!

WAILING? I CALL IT SINGING!

In 1966, the name of the island Selkirk lived on was changed to Robinson Crusoe Island.

Surf and turf

Fish was a plentiful source of food, but it gave Selkirk tummy problems, so he ate crayfish instead. Eventually Selkirk grew so nimble running barefoot on the hills of the island that he could chase down wild goats. He used the meat to prepare a hearty broth with wild turnips, watercress and cabbage palm, seasoned with black pimento pepper.

WHAT I WOULDN'T GIVE FOR A SANDWICH!

Robinson Crusoe Island

FRIEND OR FOE

Though he prayed for rescue, Selkirk also feared seeing a boat – in case it was crewed by Spanish sailors, who tortured prisoners and turned them into slaves. Selkirk once hid from a Spanish search party by climbing a tree.

NOVEL HERO

Published in 1719, Daniel Defoe's *The Life and Strange Surprizing Adventures of Robinson Crusoe* is one of the most famous adventure stories in English literature. It is not known if Defoe and Selkirk ever met, but the author would certainly have heard of Selkirk's adventures and few would dispute that he used the tales as inspiration for his novel.

ADVENTURES OF ROBINSON CRUSOE BY DANIEL DE FOE

"MY BOAT"

Selkirk was rescued in 1709.

WANT MORE?

Learn more ☆ www.smithsonianmag.com/history-archaeology/crusoe.html

COST YOU AN ARM AND A LEG

The Incas started off as a small tribe in what is now Peru, and established an empire that stretched across South America from Colombia to Argentina. Known as fearsome warriors, they used intimidation and humiliation as part of their warfare. One of their tactics was to capture and kill the enemy's leaders – then turn them into artefacts for display.

Beating their enemies
The Incas killed and flayed some of their enemies, then used the skin to make a drum called a *runa tinya*.

DRINKS GO TO MY HEAD

An enemy's skull may have been covered in gold and used as a cup for drinking an Inca brew called *chichi*.

IT'S NOTHING TO SMILE ABOUT!

Bone of contention

Shin bones were made into musical flutes by removing the soft marrow and drilling holes along the length.

GOING OUT WITH A BANG

Sometimes the stomach was used to form a drum, while the arms and head were left to hang over it, almost as if the dead person was playing drums on himself.

Royal blood... bones, teeth and skin

A famous Incan traitor, called Rumiñahui, killed Illescas, son of the Inca ruler Huayna Capac, and made panpipes from his bones. His teeth were strung into a necklace.

Inca soldiers preparing for battle

MARCHING BAND

Upon the attack signal in battle, a line of Incas would march towards the enemy playing human war drums and bone flutes. This moving, musical wall of terror showed the enemy their fate – should they be defeated in battle.

WANT MORE?

www.kidskonnect.com/subjectindex/16-educational/history/255-ancient-inca.html

BEETLE MANIA

Brazil's love affair with the German-designed Volkswagen Beetle began when the first shipment of 30 arrived from Germany in 1950. Brazilian production of the car began three years later, ending finally in 1996. However, the country won't let them die. The roads are still over-run with them. Brazil is keeping this classic little car on life support.

CAUGHT THE BUG

Beetles are especially popular in the towns of Cunha, Goiás and Pirenopolinos, where they are found at every crossroads, traffic lights and in every supermarket car park. Cunha's population of 21,874 people owns 2230 Beetles. This works out at one Beetle for every ten people.

Beetles are everywhere.

People's car

Brazilian people are sentimental about their Beetles, but there are also practical reasons for owning one. Volkswagen, which means 'people's car' in German, built them to be affordable. They are very basic, which means they are reliable and easy to maintain. The suspension system survives longer than that of other cars on the steep and bumpy cobble-stoned streets of the small towns.

Second home

Back in 1953, Volkswagen opened the first of many factories outside of Germany, in Sao Paulo in Brazil. The factory, which was the second-largest VW factory in the world, simply assembled parts imported from Germany. Production stopped in 1986.

Volkswagen assembly line, Sao Paulo, Brazil

Franco in the driving seat

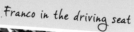

THESE WILL HAVE THE COUNTRY.

Presidential reprieve

In 1993, the president of Brazil, Itamar Franco, restarted the production of the Beetle as a way of creating jobs in the country, which was suffering severe economic problems. The assembly lines were finally shut down in 1996, when the economy picked up, and the well-off people began to buy more expensive new cars.

BEETLE JUICE

During the world oil crisis in the 1970s, when the car market crashed, Beetles continued to roll off the production line in Brazil. VW simply converted the engine of the Beetle to run on ethanol, a fuel made from sugar cane – a crop that is plentiful in Brazil.

Sugar cane

WANT MORE?

VW Beetle cars are known as *Fusca* in Brazil.

CROAKED!

Poison dart frogs, from South and Central America, might look pretty harmless but they are highly poisonous. Some secrete deadly poison, while others are less dangerous. They are called 'dart frogs' because native peoples of South America, such as the Choco Emberá peoples of Colombia, use the poison on the tips of the darts they hunt with. These brightly-coloured amphibians belong to a family of frogs called *Dendrobatidae*.

WARNING
MOST DANGEROUS OF THE TOXIC THREE!

Kokoe poison dart frog

THIS DROP COULD KILL TWO ELEPHANTS!

Poison dart frogs secrete the poison from their skin.

THE TOXIC THREE

Of the more than 175 species of poison dart frogs, only three are toxic enough to be used on a blowgun dart. These are the golden poison frog, the black-legged dart frog and the kokoe poison dart frog. The golden poison frog is by far the most poisonous – just one drop of its secretions is toxic enough to kill 20 humans.

One that gets away

The Choco Emberá peoples do not kill the golden poison frog to get its poison. They scrape the dart on the frog's back, which releases the deadly fluid. Once the toxin has been harvested, the frogs are allowed to hop away.

ANY ANIMAL THAT EATS ME WILL DIE!

Golden poison frog

50

The number of dart tips that can be poisoned with the secretions of one frog.

Blowguns are made from palm wood.

Horrible harvest

The black-legged dart frog and the kokoe poison dart frog are held over a fire on sticks, until they become distressed and release their poison. At first, white bubbles come out. When dried, this can make dart tips deadly for about a year. Then, a yellow substance is secreted, which remains poisonous for about two years.

Well blow me down!

The blowguns used by the Choco Emberá peoples are about 3m (9ft) long. They are used to shoot animals, such as monkeys, high up in trees. Just a few seconds after one has been shot, the creature falls to the ground with a thump.

WANT MORE?

Golden poison frog — www.thejunglestore.com/Golden-Poison-Frog-Facts

A FLAVOUR OF THE SALAR DE UYUNI

Salar de Uyuni, in Bolivia, is the world's largest salt flat. Sitting 3653m (11,985ft) above sea level, and covering an area half the size of Belgium, it was formed 40,000 years ago when a lake evaporated and left behind the layer of salt. In some places the salt is 6m (20ft) thick.

> ANYWHERE TO STAY AROUND HERE?

For well-seasoned travellers
How do you accommodate tourists when you are surrounded by nothing but salt? You build a hotel from it, of course! This is precisely what a number of hoteliers have done in the Salar de Uyuni.

Causing a stink
In the past, some salt hotels were built far out on the plain, where there is no access to drains. Toilet waste was released into the environment, causing damage. This has left a bad taste in the mouths of locals keen to protect the plain. Nowadays, new salt hotels are only allowed on the edges of the salt plain, where there are proper sanitation systems.

Tasteful furniture
You may have heard of table salt, but what about salt tables? Most of the furniture in the hotels is made of salt, including the tables, beds and chairs.

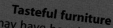

A sitting room made of salt

Island in a sea of salt

Jutting above the flat white sea of salt is a rocky island called Isla Incahuasi. It is peppered with gigantic cacti. There are also unusual and fragile coral-like structures and deposits that often consist of fossils and algae. The island is the remains of the top of an ancient volcano.

Isla Incahuasi

ONLY ANOTHER 24,000 TONNES TO GO!

Three species of flamingo visit the region each year to breed.

You might find a salt cellar
Some local people make a living from selling souvenirs made of salt.

Grinding out a living

Until the recent tourist boom in the region, the only human inhabitants of the chilly, harsh region were salt miners. They still come today, extracting about 25,000 tonnes (27,558 tons) of salt each year.

Salt mining and tourism are the biggest industries in the desert.

WANT MORE?

There are 10 billion tonnes (11 billion tons) of salt in the desert.

EVITA ON TOUR

> DON'T CRY FOR ME, ARGENTINA.

Eva Perón was a legend in her own lifetime. She was the wife of the Argentinian President from 1946 until her death in 1952, and had an almost saint-like status among her people. Even in death Eva, also known as Evita, remained popular. Her body was preserved and put on public display, where it was revered as a relic. When the military government overthrew Evita's husband in 1955, they made her body 'disappear'.

Final makeover

Dr Pedro Ara began embalming the first lady's corpse within hours of her death. While Ara prepared Eva's body for lying in state, her hairstylist dyed her hair blond one last time, and her personal manicurist painted her fingernails with clear polish.

NAIL Polish

> SHE WAS ONLY 33 YEARS OLD.

13

The number of days members of the public filed past Evita's body as it lay in state.

Dying to see her

The lines to visit Evita's body in the Argentine Confederation of Labour building stretched in all directions around city blocks in Buenos Aires. Eight people lost their lives in a crush to see the late first lady.

Global odyssey

Between 1955 and 1957, Evita's body was hidden all over Buenos Aires. She was left inside a van parked beside the city's waterworks and behind a cinema. She spent some time in the attic of the military intelligence building. Word of every location leaked to the public, who created shrines with burning candles and flowers near each hiding place.

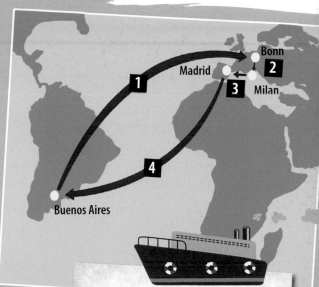

Body snatchers

In 1971, supporters of Evita's husband assassinated General Aramburu, the person who had ordered the theft of Evita's body, then kidnapped his body. They held it to ransom until Evita's body was returned to her husband in Spain.

THEY SHOULD WRITE A SONG ABOUT HER.

1957: Taken by ship from Buenos Aires to Bonn, Germany. Buried in the garden of the Argentinian ambassador's residence.

1958: Taken to Italy and buried in a cemetery in Milan under a false name.

1971: Body dug up and flown to Spain, where it is put on display in her husband's home.

1974: Juan Perón dies and his wife's body is returned to Buenos Aires, and displayed briefly.

1976: Buried in Recoleta Cemetery, Buenos Aires.

Evita's tomb in Buenos Aires

Resting in peace and security

In 1976, Evita was finally laid to rest in the Recoleta Cemetery of Buenos Aires. Her tomb was built by a company that specialized in making bank vaults, and was built to resist tomb raiders. As an extra security precaution, Evita's sister was given the only key.

WANT MORE?

A biography ☆ www.movies.uip.de/evita/eva/EvaBio.html

SAILOR'S GRAVEYARD

The waters off
Cape Horn, the southernmost
tip of South America, are notoriously
dangerous. Since ships began to round
the Horn about 400 years ago, the
route has been considered a
milestone in a sailor's career.
Any sailor lucky enough
to round the Horn
safely never forgets
the experience.

Savage seas
The waters are awash
with sailing hazards –
icebergs that drift up from
Antarctica, lashing storms,
strong currents and
driving winds that whip
up giant waves. Countless
vessels have been sunk,
sending many sailors
to a watery grave.

MAN
OVERBOARD!

Rogue waves up
to the height of
a ten-storey
building can
appear without
warning.

HOLD ON, WE'RE ALMOST THERE.

The long way round
Before the Panama Canal was completed in 1914, ships had to round the Horn to move goods or people from the Atlantic side of North and South America to the Pacific side. If the weather conditions were bad, the voyage could take up to eight months.

Sailors were often swept overboard.

RIGHTS OF PASSAGE

Traditionally, sailors who rounded the Horn were entitled to wear a gold hoop earring in their left ear, and were allowed to dine with one foot on the table. A sailor who had also rounded the Cape of Good Hope, at the southern end of Africa, could place both feet on the table.

Cape Horn

Blowing their own horn club
Today, sailors who go round the Horn on a non-stop voyage of more than 5556km (3452mi) can become members of the International Association of Cape Horners. The original members were professional seamen serving on clipper ships in the 1800s. Nowadays, members include crews from several famous Round the World Yacht races.

WANT MORE?

Cape Horn weather ☆ www.mountain-forecast.com/peaks/Cape-Horn/metar

PIRANHA ATTACK!

In the movies, when someone falls into a South American river, piranha fish attack with shocking ferocity. Within seconds, the bubbling water turns red and a stripped skeleton bobs to the surface. This image has made the piranha one of the most feared predators in the world, but just how deadly is it?

Temperamental about temperature
Piranhas live in warm, low-lying South American rivers with a temperature of 24–30°C (75–86°F). They can't survive in temperatures outside this range.

BITE TO EAT

Piranha fish have razor-sharp, serrated teeth, which lock together for maximum cutting effect. Snapping quickly and continuously, a piranha strips the flesh off a bone in seconds.

I'M SO HUNGRY, I COULD EAT AN APPLE!

Fish supper
It's true that piranhas attack creatures much larger than themselves, but this is usually when the prey is injured and bleeding. The piranha's reputation as a man-eater has been highly exaggerated. In fact, many piranha species would rather eat fruit than meat.

WE GET A TERRIBLE PRESS, YOU KNOW.

River health squad

Piranhas do have their uses. Every year, extreme tides force a giant wave, up to 8m (26ft) high, up the Amazon River. Known as *pororoca*, it kills many animals, which would rot and cause diseases if piranhas didn't devour their remains.

A piranha caught on a fisherman's hook may be attacked by other piranhas from its shoal.

Pororoca wave

BLOOD IN THE WATER EXCITES THEM TO MADNESS.

BAD PR

The piranha may have got its savage reputation in 1913, when US president Theodore Roosevelt visited the Amazon. To entertain the president, a bleeding cow was dumped into a pool filled with starving piranhas. The president was stunned by the feeding frenzy that followed. Tales of the terrifying flesh-eating fish soon spread around the world.

Theodore Roosevelt

WANT MORE?

Video ☆ channel.nationalgeographic.com/channel/videos/piranha-bite-force/

HELL ON EARTH

St Joseph Island

Royale Island

Devil's Island

Devil's Island was once feared as the toughest prison on Earth. Located in French Guiana, the prison system was famous for its brutality. Out of the 80,000 French convicts imprisoned there between 1852 and 1953, only 2000 came out alive. Most of the others died from disease or from the brutal conditions. Many were driven insane.

Devil by name
Devil's Island, along with two other island jails and prisons on the mainland, formed the prison colony. Devil's Island held the most famous of the inmates and so became the most well-known prison in the system. Over time, the entire colony became known as Devil's Island.

TWO JAILORS
The islands were almost impossible to escape. They were defended by guards, the seas were shark-infested, the rivers were full of piranhas, and the jungle teemed with army ants and alligators.

Devourer of men

Troublemakers were put in solitary confinement on St Joseph Island, known as the 'devourer of men'. Inmates were left in tiny, pitch-black cells and were forbidden to speak.

Vampire victim

The most famous inmate was a political prisoner called Captain Alfred Dreyfus. He spent 11 years in the prison before being pardoned in 1906. He later wrote about the brutal conditions. In one tale, he describes how he was chained up at night, making him easy prey to vampire bats.

I WAS FRAMED.

Road to nowhere

Some of the convicts were given the pointless task of building a road that would never be used. Nicknamed Route Zero by the prisoners, the road reached a distance of 25km (15.5mi) after 40 years of hard work.

Hell's bells

When the prisons were open, sharks were common around the islands because bodies were regularly tossed into the sea after funerals. The sharks, knowing what was coming, would begin to circle when they heard the church bell.

To hell and back

Henri Charrière wrote about his daring escape from Devil's Island in a book called *Papillon*. Charrière claims that he and a companion leapt into the choppy seas and floated to the mainland on coconut-filled sacks. But the French authorities claim he was never imprisoned on the island.

WANT MORE?

The story of Charrière's escape from Devil's Island was made into a film in 1973.

DESERT DWELLERS

The Atacama Desert is the driest place on Earth. There are parts where rainfall has never been recorded. Yet more than a million people live there, and manage to make a living. It seems almost impossible. All living things need water, so where do the inhabitants of this dry, desolate land get the water they need?

Mummified cow

Dry as a bone
Without moisture, nothing rots. Everything turns into an artifact in the Atacama Desert. Animals are mummified naturally where they fall and die.

Water palaver!
Some villages have water trucked in to the desert, or piped in from hundreds of kilometres away. This makes the water very expensive.

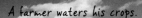

A farmer waters his crops.

Greening the desert
Determined farmers in the far north of the desert grow olives, tomatoes and cucumbers. They water the plants with water extracted from underground rock. People living in the high plains of the Altiplano water crops from streams formed from melted mountain snow.

Nature knows best
Cold air coming off the Pacific Ocean cools the hot desert air to produce a blanket of fog, known as *camanchaca*. This is pushed inland by winds from the sea. As the fog hits cacti, the vapour turns into liquid water. The droplets are a vital source of water for some desert animals, as well as the cactus itself.

Fog catchers
Some Atacaman desert villages copy nature to capture water from the fog. Fine nets are hung above troughs on top of hills. As the fog condenses on the surface of the nets, the moisture drips into the troughs. Pipes carry the water down to the village.

AH, A FEW MORE DROPS FOR THE BEANS.

Fog nets in Atacama

10,000
Litres of water captured each day by nets in the village of Chungungo, Chile.

Water collected from the fog catchers has allowed people to develop small gardens.

Mummified child

I WANT MY MUMMY!

WANT MORE?

SANDS OF TIME

Despite the hostile conditions, people have been living in the Atacama Desert since well before 7000BC. We know this because human-made mummified bodies from this time have been recovered from the region. The remains are 4000 years older than the oldest Egyptian mummies.

Find out more ☆ www.universetoday.com/48164/atacama-desert

LIQUID RAINBOW

The Caño Cristales, in Colombia, is one of the most beautiful rivers in the world. It is nicknamed the 'Liquid Rainbow' because for a short period between June and November each year, its crystal-clear waters are spectacularly transformed by a vibrant explosion of natural colours.

SEEING RED

A little red aquatic plant, called *Macarenia clavigera*, is responsible for the river's magical transformation. When it blossoms, it creates a red carpet which is offset by yellow sand and a variety of colours produced by algae, corals and the rocky riverbed.

Flower power

In the wet season, the deep water means the *Macarenia clavigera* don't get enough sunshine to turn red. In the dry season, there isn't enough water to feed the plants. Between the wet and dry seasons, the water level drops enough for the sun to warm the plants and algae, causing the river to burst into life.

Giant kettles
Circular pits in the riverbed, known as 'giant kettles', are carved out by fragments of rock carried in the swirling water. The pits are always growing. Each one adds a dramatic shape to the river, as well as providing colour contrast to the plant-life.

In the news
The journalist and explorer Andrés Hurtado García made the river world-famous when he wrote about it in a Colombian newspaper in the 1980s.

Beauty and the beast
Caño Cristales's annual show could be a sell-out, but tourists mostly stay away. This is because the region in which it flows is a haven for terrorists and drug traffickers. Nowadays, the Colombian army patrols the area, so the bad guys could soon be on their way out.

A succession of rapids and waterfalls

WANT MORE?

More pictures ☆ http://intactnature.com/cano-cristales-colombia

IT TAKES TWO

The Argentine tango is a dramatic dance, with a 'leader' and a 'follower'. The leader suggests where the follower should step, but it is up to the follower whether to go there or not. Throughout the dance, partners hold each other in a close embrace.

The tango began as a dance that complete strangers could perform.

> WHY ARE YOU LAUGHING, DARLING?

> YOUR MOUSTACHE IS TICKLING MY NOSE!

> DO I KNOW YOU?

Humble beginnings
The tango originated in the working-class areas of Buenos Aires in Argentina and Montevideo in Uruguay in the 1880s. Spanish settlers mixed with Uruguayan and African immigrants, and all influenced the style of the dance.

Going up-market
The dance spread to the ballrooms of Europe and then New York in the 1920s. The tango quickly became as popular as the foxtrot and the Charleston.

Street tango dancers

Putting on the moves

While the leader subtly guides the follower, the dancers' feet glide smoothly across the ground. Quick steps, turns, lunges and suggestive flicks of a high-heeled foot add a dramatic flourish to the dance.

Let's play the music and dance

Tango is danced to a repetitive, moody style of music. This is usually played on a violin or the *bandoneon*, which is a type of accordion.

A bandoneon

WANT MORE?

Find out more ☆ http://users.skynet.be/fa550465/content/tango/glossary.html

ALIVE AND KICKING

In 1972, Uruguayan Air Force Flight 571 vanished crossing the Andes. The plane's passengers included a Uruguayan rugby team, along with relatives and friends. With no sign of the plane, the search was abandoned after eight days. About 62 days later, two of the passengers surfaced, bringing news that there were survivors who needed rescuing.

Sixteen people survived the crash.

WE ARE SAVED!

Refuselage
To escape from the freezing temperatures, the survivors huddled inside the wrecked plane. Gaping holes were plugged with luggage and unzipped seat covers were used for bedding.

AVALANCHE!

An avalanche crashed down the mountain 17 days after the accident, covering the plane with snow. Eight people were unable to dig their way out and suffocated.

Life or death decision
For the first few days, the passengers ate chocolate bars, sweets and snacks found in the plane. But they soon ran out. With no other food available, the group made the extremely difficult decision to eat the flesh of people who had died in the crash.

Water into wine bottles

To get drinking water, the survivors melted snow and collected it drop-by-drop in empty wine bottles.

Do or die

Sixty-one days after the crash, three men set off to get help. Two days into the journey, one of them returned to the plane wreck. The other men trudged for 10 days in Arctic conditions before finally spotting a livestock herder, who went to the nearest town to alert rescuers.

HELP! WE'RE DOWN HERE!

Most of the passengers were students.

Search and rescue, and rescue

On 22 December 1972, two search-and-rescue helicopters arrived at the crash scene. Due to conditions on the ground, only six survivors were taken away. The rescue team and the other survivors were left behind, and rescued the following day.

Survivors fighting to stay alive.

In the news

A transistor radio found in the wreckage kept the survivors up-to-date with world news. Eight days after the crash, they heard a devastating report that the search was off. Weeks later, they learned that the two men who had gone to seek help had found it.

WANT MORE?

A film based on the crash was released in 1993.

LOST CITY OF GOLD

For hundreds of years from the 1540s, adventurers tried to find El Dorado: a lost city built of gold and jewels which is likely to never have existed. El Dorado, meaning 'Gilded One' in Spanish, was more likely a name for the leader (known as the Zipa) of the Muisca tribe, which lived in the highlands of an area that is now in Colombia.

The mythical, golden city of El Dorado

GOLD IS DEFINITELY YOUR COLOUR!

Gold dust being blown over the body of the king

MAN OF GOLD

Each new Zipa went through an initiation ceremony that involved being covered in gold dust. This is probably what Spanish adventurers, called conquistadores, were referring to when they first used the name El Dorado in the early 1500s.

Gold for the gods
The new Zipa was also taken out into the middle of a lake, called Guatavita, where he threw gold and jewels into the water as offerings to the gods. The Zipa then dived in and the spectators threw gold and gems in after him.

Golden statue of the Zipa's raft

I FEEL DIZZY!

PALES INTO INSIGNIFICANCE

In 1545, conquistadores Lázaro Fonte and Hernán Perez de Quesada hired labourers to drain the lake, so that they could retrieve the treasure. After three months, the lake had been lowered by 3m (9.8ft). Only a small amount of gold was recovered. It had a value of 3000 to 4000 pesos, which is worth about £65,000 (US$100,000) today.

THERE'S A HOLE IN MY BUCKET ...

DON'T BANK ON IT!

In the 1580s, a rich merchant, Antonio de Sepúlveda, used 8000 local people to cut a great notch into the high banks of the lake. The water drained away, dropping the water level by about 20m (65ft), but the bank collapsed, killing many of the labourers. That was the end of that scheme!

Stuck in the mud

The last attempt to drain the lake was in 1898, when a group from London dug a tunnel that opened up in the centre of the lake. The water drained away, but left behind slimy mud that was impossible to walk over. The sun soon baked the mud like cement, sealing in the treasure. The workers found just £500 (US$775) worth of gold – less than was spent recovering it.

WANT MORE?

HOW DO I GET TO MOMPÓS TOWN CENTRE?

NO IDEA! NEVER HEARD OF IT!

'THE TOWN THAT TIME FORGOT'

NO SUPERMARKETS HERE, THANK YOU VERY MUCH!

Stuck on an island in the middle of marshland, the Colombian town of Mompós is pretty difficult to get to. Most Colombian people don't even know it exists – yet this sleepy little town was once the third-most important city in the country. Founded in 1540, Mompós thrived in the Spanish colonial era because of its island location in the middle of the Magdalena River. This waterway was a vital trade route linking the Caribbean Sea and the country's interior.

DRIED-UP RIVER TRADE

Up until the 19th century, the riverbank alongside the city was packed with large boats, and the streets were full of workers transporting tobacco, precious metals, contraband and slaves. Since then the boats have downsized and there are far fewer of them. These days they deliver goods for the town's inhabitants, and the once bustling streets are now tranquil.

Colonial copies

The city's historic wealth is obvious from the architecture, which is distinctly Spanish in style. Grand squares lined with the homes of the wealthy grew out of whitewashed streets.

Santa Domingo church in Mompós

Worth a mint

Mompós was once home to a royal mint, where rich traders stored precious metals and jewels, safe from Caribbean pirates.

TIME CAPSULE

The city's magnificent colonial architecture has remained pretty much unchanged. There was no need to knock down buildings to make multi-storey car parks, as there are hardly any cars – donkeys and carts are still the main form of transport. The population of about 30,000 isn't large enough to need chain stores, so most of the buildings are still used for their original purpose.

WANT MORE?

Learn more ★ whc.unesco.org/en/list/742

COFFEE REPUBLIC

Coffee is native to Ethiopia in Africa, and came to Brazil only in 1727. By the start of the 1830s, however, Brazil had become the world's top coffee producer, and was exporting 600,000 bags of the stuff each year. From 1830 to 1964, coffee was Brazil's main export. This innocent-looking bean has had a huge influence on Brazilian life, including its politics, its people and of course its economy.

2.6 million
Tonnes of green coffee are produced in Brazil each year.

Coffee steamer
In the 1870s and 1880s, railways were built across Brazil so that coffee for export could be transported easily to the ports.

Coffee presidents
From 1894, Brazil's presidents all came from the coffee-producing states of Sao Paulo and Minas Gerais. This was no coincidence – only a few privileged people were allowed to vote, and they voted to protect their interests.

UNFAIR TRADE

After 1929 the world was gripped by an economic depression. Demand for Brazilian coffee collapsed. The government tried to help plantation owners by buying the coffee they could not sell. Ordinary Brazilians were unhappy with this and there was a revolution. After months of violence the army intervened and installed Getulio Vargas as president in 1937.

Revolutionaries burn furniture in the street during protests in 1937

A BLEND OF PEOPLE

In the first half of the 19th century, 1.5 million African slaves were brought in to Brazil to work on the coffee plantations. When the slave trade was finally abolished in Brazil in 1850, the plantation owners took on immigrants from Italy, Portugal and Germany to do the work. From 1877 to 1903, almost two million immigrants arrived.

The coffee industry depended on African slaves.

I WANT A CUP OF TEA!

HARVESTING

The coffee is harvested from June to September. The bright red, firm berries are stripped from the tree along with other plant matter, which is removed by tossing everything into the air and allowing the wind to carry away sticks and leaves. The heavier berries fall back into the harvester's sieve.

WANT MORE?

Learn more ☆ www.coffeeresearch.org/coffee/brazil.htm

FLOATING ISLANDS

Dotting the western corner of Lake Titicaca, Peru, are what appear to be giant corn-coloured lily pads – some half the size of a football pitch. These are the Islas Flotantes, which translates as 'floating islands'. Made from rushes, they do exactly as their name suggests, and are home to a tribe of South American people called the Uros.

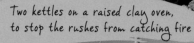

Two kettles on a raised clay oven, to stop the rushes from catching fire

UROS V INCAS

Centuries ago, the small Uros tribe came up with the idea of creating and living on man-made islands to isolate and protect themselves from rival tribes, including the Collas and the Incas.

Bundles of totora, used for building the islands.

Floating Uros Island boats made from totora bundles

ISLAND BUILDING

The *totora* is a cattail-type rush growing in the lake. Its dense roots support the top layer, which rots and must be replaced regularly by stacking more rushes on top. The Uros people harvest the rushes in the shallows of the lake, bundle them together tightly and use them to make the platforms, their houses and canoes.

Densely-packed rushes at the edge of an island

Fire hazard
Cooking fires are built on a layer of stones to protect the rushes.

A larger island, housing about ten families

MORE PEOPLE, MORE ISLAND

The islands change in size, and more are created as the need arises. The larger islands house about ten families, while smaller ones – about 30m (98ft) wide – house only two or three families.

There are about 42 islands floating on Lake Titicaca.

I NEED A BIGGER

WANT MORE?

Find out more ☆ www.incatourism.com/places-to-visit-in-peru/puno-tourism

DUTY FREE

You can buy anything, from fake designer sunglasses to guns, at the stalls in the Cuidad del Este market in Paraguay. The city's location on the border of Paraguay, Brazil and Argentina makes it the ideal distribution point for all kinds of illegal items. It's hardly surprising that the city has been a hotspot for smuggling for a very long time.

Smugglers avoid paying an import tax of 60% on the price of anything costing more than US$300.

The bridge is always busy.

Friendship Bridge

BRASIL   PARAGUAY

Busy bridge
Porters can be hired to carry the goods over to Brazil using the Friendship Bridge. This links Cuidad del Este with the Brazilian town of Foz do Iguaçu. Most of Paraguay's imports and exports cross this bridge, so it gets pretty busy.

ILLEGAL PARCEL COMING DOWN!!

Parcel drop
The porters don't bother passing through customs on the Brazilian side of the bridge. This is to avoid paying import tax, or getting arrested if they're carrying anything illegal. Instead, the porters drop their packages over the side of the bridge to youngsters waiting on the riverbank below. The parcels are then sent on to the people who bought them.

HURRY!! WE ONLY HAVE 15 MINUTES!

15-MINUTE DASH

Everybody knows about the 15-minute-long custom officer changeover that takes place at the Brazilian end of the Friendship Bridge. During this time, everyone rushes into the country with their illicit goods, taking advantage of the lapse in security.

WANT MORE?

Smugglers also use underground passages that lead into Brazil and Argentina.

DANCING TO THEIR OWN TUNE

Capoeira is a Brazilian martial art that involves music and fluid acrobatic moves, as well as leg sweeps, kicks and punches. Some historians think it was developed in Africa, while others believe it was developed in the rural areas of Brazil by the African slaves and their descendants.

Disguised as a dance

Capoeira's dance-like appearance may have been a way of slaves concealing what they were really up to – practising self-defence. This hand-to-hand combat would have been useful for any slaves that managed to escape, particularly when faced with the *capitães-do-mato* – the armed and mounted men sent to hunt them down.

CLUCK, CLUCK! THEY'RE FIGHTING AGAIN.

Chicken in a basket

Capoeira may have developed just outside a large bird market in Rio de Janeiro. It was to here that slaves brought *capoeiras*, which were baskets containing live chickens, to sell. While waiting around, the slaves may have filled the time playing and developing capoeira. Its name could be a reference to their wares.

ATTACK AND DEFENCE

During a game of capoeira, called a *joga*, players use moves to attack and defend their space. Players can hit their opponent but that isn't the main purpose of play. The goal is to control the space and the other player's movements. There is no real winner or loser.

HEY, I DIDN'T TOUCH HIM.

CIRCLE ROUND

A crowd surround the players in a circle, called a *roda*. Music is played, and everyone sings and claps while the two players make moves in the centre.

Berimbau

Pandeiro

Rhythm and moves
The speed and nature of the joga are influenced by the music. The lead instrument is the *berimbau*, a one-string musical bow with a gourd at one end. There is also a drum, called an *atabaque*, and a tambourine, called a *pandeiro*. People sing along to the music to create a magical atmosphere.

Atabaque

WANT MORE?

Learn more ☆ www.capoeira.bz/mestreacordeon/capoeira/capoeira.html

A NEW SOUTH WALES

In 1865, a group of Welsh settlers established Y Wladfa Gymreig in the Chubut Valley of Patagonia, Argentina. The settlement, whose name translates as Welsh Colony, survives to this day. It is estimated that there are now 50,000 people of Welsh descent living in Argentina, many of whom speak the Welsh language.

The Argentinian government gave the Welsh settlers land along the Chubut River in Patagonia.

LOOKS LIKE SUNSHINE AGAIN!

Welsh professor
A Welsh colony in South America was the brain-child of Professor Michael D. Jones, a Welsh preacher based in Bala in Wales. He called for a new 'little Wales beyond Wales'.

THE MIMOSA

FARE
LIVERPOOL TO PATAGONIA
- - - - - - - -
£12 ADULTS
£6 CHILDREN

SETTING SAIL

On 27 July 1865, 153 Welsh settlers arrived aboard the converted tea-clipper *Mimosa*. The *Mimosa* had cost £2500 (US$3860) to hire and convert to passenger use, and the fare from Liverpool to Patagonia was £12 (US$19) for adults and £6 (US$9) for children.

Home from home?

The settlers had been told that the area was like lowland Wales, which is lush and green. Instead they found a parched landscape, with little food, water or shelter. According to legend, the settlers slept in caves, before setting off with their belongings in a single wheelbarrow.

Language revival

Over the years, use of the Welsh language declined, and there was little contact between Wales and Chubut. This changed in 1965 when a large number of Welsh people visited Patagonia to celebrate the 100th anniversary of the colony. Since then, there has been a dramatic increase in the number of visitors from Wales.

These days, knowing the language is considered cool – even among people who are not of Welsh ancestry.

Tea time

Descendants of the Welsh settlers still observe some Welsh cultural activities, including afternoon tea.

Not without rugby!

In 2006, the links between the Chubut Valley and Wales were again strengthened, when the Welsh national rugby team arrived in the region to play the first game of a two-test tour of Argentina.

Tea houses serve tea and cakes.

WANT MORE?

The Wales Argentina Society ☆ www.cymru-ariannin.com

In the 16th century, many South American natives died from diseases brought over from Europe. One of the most devastating was smallpox. Starting in Hispaniola in December 1518, it swept through Mexico, Colombia and Venezuela. By the end of 1527, the epidemic had reached Peru, where it played a key role in the conquering of the Incan Empire.

POXY IMPORT

Huayna Capac

No immunity
Unlike the Spanish, the Incas had not developed an immunity to smallpox, so when it hit people died in their thousands.

An Inca road

ROAD TO RUIN
One reason why smallpox spread so quickly through the Incan Empire was that it was carried along the Inca road system, which consisted of two roads that linked the whole empire. Many people travelled on the roads, infecting others everywhere they went.

Over 200,000 Incas died of smallpox, cutting the population by half.

King killer

In 1528, smallpox killed the much-loved Incan emperor Huayna Capac. The people became divided in their support between his two sons, Atahualpa and Huascar, and a civil war broke out. Not only was smallpox killing the population, but the people were killing each other too.

I THINK I'LL HAVE THIS PLACE!

Conquistador Francisco Pizarro

STAY BACK. I'VE GOT THE POX!

DIVIDED THEY FALL

The political instability among the Incans made it easier for them to be conquered in the 1530s. It is said that it took just 168 men, led by a conquistador called Francisco Pizarro, to seize the entire empire, which was the size of Spain and Italy combined.

Scary gods

The Inca warriors thought the Spanish conquistadores were savage gods. They'd never seen horses, guns, white skin and shining armour before. But scariest of all was the fearful disease which the Spanish seemed to be immune to.

Until Europeans arrived in South America, it was free of smallpox, typhus, cholera, measles and many other infectious diseases.

I AM A GOD, I AM A GOD...

The conquistadores were brutal.

WANT MORE?

Learn more ☆ http://incas.mrdonn.org/spanisharrival.html

WHAT'S THE FUTSAL?

Ever wondered how South America manages to produce so many brilliant football players, such as Robinho, Ronaldo, Ronaldinho and Neymar? Well, look no further than futsal, an indoor five-a-side football game that was developed to be played on a basketball court.

The name futsal is a combination of the Spanish words futbol, which means football, and sala, which means hall.

Ronaldinho

ARGH, MY LEG!

I DIDN'T TOUCH HIM

ORIGINS

The game was invented in Uruguay, and then perfected in Brazil in the first half of the 20th century. Its popularity has spread around the globe. There have been seven Futsal World Cups – the first was held in the Netherlands in 1989. Brazil have won the trophy five times.

FIFA FUTSAL WORLD CUP

Futsal World Cup trophy

Equipment
Futsal is played with hockey-sized goals. A standard ball would be too large for the pitch and too bouncy for the polished hardwood floors, so the one used is smaller and not so bouncy.

Futsal skills

As there are only five players on each team, it is a fast-paced, frantic game. This encourages players to control the ball closely, pass it accurately, and to think quickly. Of course the players need to be physically fit too. So ordinary football, with its large pitch and extra players, isn't a problem for futsal players.

WE ARE THE CHAMPIONS!

Brazil wins the trophy in 2012.

Anytime, anywhere

The smaller size of the futsal pitch means it can squeeze into some unlikely places. The pitches can be found on the top of skyscrapers and even on an oil rig in the sea off Rio de Janeiro, Brazil.

WANT MORE?

Learn more ☆ www.thefa.com/GetIntoFootball/GetIntoFootballPages/futsal

COWBOYS OF THE SOUTHERN WORLD

In the heart of Argentina lie vast regions of grassland, called the Pampas. In the 18th century, cattle and horses roamed free in these grasslands. Horsemen known as *gauchos* lived by hunting the animals until the late 19th century, when the land was fenced off and the livestock was farmed on huge cattle ranches, known as *estancias*.

WHAT A MOOO-VING SIGHT!

HOLY WATER

Gauchos drank a brewed drink still popular in South America today, called maté. It is prepared by soaking dried leaves of *yerba mate* – a type of holly – in hot water. It is drunk through a metal straw from a calabash gourd, and is shared among friends. The end of the straw has small holes that allow in the liquid, but block out the leaves.

CAN I TRY SOME, MATE?

Born under a wandering star
The early gauchos led a nomadic life. From the 19th century, they began to settle down on the estancias, where they rounded up cattle, mended fences and branded animals.

COWBOY BOOTS

The gauchos made their own boots with the hide of a freshly killed calf. After stripping the legs of the animal, they simply pulled the skin over their legs. As the hide dried out, it formed a snug boot.

Gauchos threw a boleadora (made of stones bound in leather strips) at the legs of cattle to trip them up.

FANCY A BURGER?

Being a cowboy is a way of life for both the young and the old.

Class war

Gauchos were once looked down on as lower-class citizens. But, when the wars of independence against Spain began in 1810, the gauchos were called into military service and proved themselves on the battlefield. Today, Argentinians celebrate the gaucho contribution to the War of Independence on 16 June every year.

MEAT MEN

Gauchos ate mainly meat. They had no way of preserving food, so after a cow was butchered, they would cook all of the meat immediately over an open fire.

WANT MORE?

More info ✦ video.nationalgeographic.com/video/places/regions-places/south-america

MOVING STATUES

For hundreds of years, giant stone statues, known as *moai*, have gazed upon Easter Island in the Pacific Ocean. The Rapa Nui peoples carved the figures and positioned them around the island, transporting them up to 18km (11mi). It is not certain how the Rapa Nui managed to move the statues, but scientists have tested different ideas.

IS THIS MY BEST SIDE?

Cut from volcanic rock, the statues stand on stone platforms with their backs to the sea. There are about 900 in total.

Many of the statues end at the hips. The heads are usually one-third of the overall height.

ROCK...

Traditional stories mention the statues walking. In 2011 a 4.35 tonne (4.8 ton) concrete replica of an upright moai was moved using only the strength of 18 people and some rope. Three ropes were attached to the head. Two groups of people either side of the statue pulled on ropes, rocking it from side to side. A group at the rear steered the statue and stopped it from falling. The team managed to shuffle it 100m (328ft) in less than an hour.

Stolen friend

One moai was moved all the way to the British Museum in London. The statue, known as *Hoa Hakananai'a*, which translates as 'stolen friend', was removed from the island by the crew of HMS *Topaz* in 1868. Weighing about 4 tonnes (4.4 tons), the statue was dragged to the beach and floated out to the ship on a raft.

Easter Island (Rapa Nui) is listed as a World Heritage site.

...AND ROLL

In 1999 a team of archaeologists successfully moved a moai using logs and ropes. The statue was laid on a sledge made of large logs. Smaller logs were placed underneath to roll the sledge along. Using this method, 70 people could move a standard-sized moai in under 5 days.

BY DESIGN

The fat bellies may have helped with tilting the statues forward, and the heavy curved bases may have been designed so that the moai could be rocked from side to side.

The Dutch were the first Europeans to visit the island.

WANT MORE?

Walking statues ☆ www.youtube.com/watch?v=YpNuh-J5lgE

THE GREATEST LIGHT SHOW ON EARTH

Imagine the night skies above you were white with nonstop lightning, but without a single clap of thunder. This unique natural wonder happens on the southwest side of Lake Maracaibo in Venezuela. Known as the *Relámpago de Catatumbo* (Catatumbo Lightning), the flashes are so bright that they can sometimes be seen 320km (199mi) miles away.

COLOMBIA

CARIBBEAN SEA

Wind

Humid air

LAKE MARACAIBO

Cold wind

ANDES

N

WHO TURNED THE LIGHT ON?

Blowing hot and cold
No one knows for sure why the lightning happens. Many scientists believe it is the result of a clash between cold winds flowing down from the Andean highlands around the lake, and hot, moist air evaporating from the lake, as well as warm air from the Caribbean sea.

NOT ME!

Sailor's beacon
For centuries, sailors arriving at the Gulf of Venezuela have used the Catatumbo Lightning as a natural lighthouse, earning it the nickname *Faro de Maracaibo*, or Maracaibo Beacon.

I THINK THEY MAY HAVE SPOTTED US!

Sir Francis Drake

LIGHTS OUT
At the end of January 2010, the lightning disappeared for two whole months. It was the longest absence of the lightning in 104 years and people began to think it had gone for good. However, it did restart. Its absence has been put down to a drought in the region that year.

Lightning response
The lightning is said to have prevented a nighttime attack on the Spanish city of Maracaibo by English sea captain Sir Francis Drake in 1595. The flashes allowed a watchman to see Drake's ships and warn the military.

FACTS IN A FLASH
The Catatumbo Lightning forms a voltage arc more than 5km (3mi) high. It happens between 140 to 160 times a year, producing an average of 280 lightning flashes per minute over a period of seven hours.

WANT MORE?

www.wondermondo.com/Countries/SA/VEN/Zulia/Catatumbo.html

TRAPPED!

On 5 August 2010 part of the San José copper mine in Chile collapsed trapping 33 men under the ground. Nobody knew if the men were alive or dead for 17 days. Then a note from the miners was found attached to a probe that had been sent down a borehole to seek for signs of life. It took more than two months for the miners to be brought back to the surface.

Message in a borehole

Messages from relatives, food and medical supplies were passed down the borehole in special tubes. These were nicknamed *palomas*, which translates as doves.

Beam me up!

Cameras and communication equipment sent down to the miners allowed them to speak to their families. They also provided the rescuers with video updates on conditions in the mine.

HAVE YOU FED THE DOG?

HAVE YOU CLEANED YOUR TEETH?

TRY, TRY AND TRY AGAIN

Rescuers decided the best way to get the men out was to drill a shaft and winch them to the surface.
Three types of drilling equipment were used to make three different holes at the same time. This way they could be sure of success with at least one of the shafts.

Not much space capsule

The miners were brought up the shaft one-by-one in *Fenix 2* – a specially made steel capsule. It was only 54cm (21in) wide and was a tight squeeze. Once they were safely inside the capsule, the miners were hauled up at a rate of 1 metre per second (2.2mph), and took under 18 minutes to reach the surface.

AT LAST! FRESH AIR!

The rescue capsule had communication equipment, a supply of oxygen and retractable wheels to help it move through the shaft.

CHILE

All 33 miners were rescued in fairly good health.

MONITORING THE MINERS

Each miner wore a device called a bio-harness during the ascent. This monitored his heart rate, breathing, temperature and oxygen consumption. The miners also wore sunglasses because their eyes had grown unused to sunlight.

WANT MORE?

In the news ☆ www.bbc.co.uk/news/world-latin-america-11469025

LOST AND FOUND

In 1911 Yale professor Hiram Bingham discovered Machu Picchu, the lost city of the Incas. Although the city is commonly described as 'lost', it never was. It is possible that Bingham wasn't even the first Westerner to visit the site.

Local knowledge
A local guide, called Melchor Artega, led Bingham to the site. Most local people knew about the city, with some even using the terraces for growing crops.

Hiram Bingham at camp

I CLAIM THIS CITY AS MY OWN!

Highland retreat
For years, scientists wondered what Machu Picchu was. Was it a city, a mountain fortress, a religious shrine or a royal palace? Many archaeologists now agree that it was a holiday retreat for Inca royalty.

Flush with cash
Bingham was such a successful explorer that he had no trouble finding funds for his 1911 expedition. The Research Committee of the National Geographic Society made him a grant of £6420 (US$10,000). This figure was matched by Yale University.

2430m
(1.5mi)
Machu Picchu stands at this height above sea level.

View of Machu Picchu

Credit where it's due
Bingham might not have discovered Machu Picchu, but he did uncover the now-famous structures, which were overgrown after four centuries of disuse. He also recorded details, as well as mapping and photographing the site over several years.

Pipped to the post?
Some historians believe that German adventurer Augusto Berns visited Machu Picchu about 40 years before Bingham. Others claim that Peruvian explorers Enrique Palma, Gabino Sanchez and Agustín Lizarraga went to the site in 1901. And two missionaries, Thomas Payne and Stuart McNairn, may have trekked there in 1906, five years before Bingham.

READ ALL ABOUT IT
The entire April 1913 issue of National Geographic was devoted to Bingham's so-called discovery. Bingham also wrote about it in Inca Land: Explorations in the Highlands of Peru (1922) and Lost City of the Incas, a 1948 best-seller.

MACHU PICCHU

MACHU PICCHU

SKELETAL REMAINS

Yale unlocks the artefacts
For almost a century, Yale University's Peabody Museum held thousands of artefacts recovered from Machu Picchu by Bingham. After years of talks about ownership of the items, Yale finally returned them to Peru in December 2011. Among the artefacts were human bones.

WANT MORE?

More ☆ http://travel.nationalgeographic.co.uk/travel/world-heritage/machu-picchu

FOUL FOWL

The hoatzin isn't hard to miss. It smells like manure and looks like a startled punk rocker. It can fly for only about 20 seconds at a time, and has a clumsy walk. It doesn't use camouflage to hide. It isn't a predator, or a scavenger, and it doesn't eat seeds or nuts. So, just how does the hoatzin bird survive?

Hoatzins live in marshland and mangrove swamps in northern South America.

IT WASN'T ME!

HE WHO SMELT IT DEALT IT!

PARP!

CAUSING A STINK

Unlike most other birds, the hoatzin eats leaves. It has a special crop (the first part of the food canal), that has two folds to digest the fibre of the leaves – rather like a cow does with its first stomach. It's a slow process but it means the hoatzin can eat lots of plants that other birds can't. The downside is that hoatzins produce smelly farts, earning them the nickname stink bird.

The hoatzin is the national bird of Guyana.

TWO LEFT WINGS

The hoatzin's large digestive system leaves little room for a good-sized breast bone or flight muscles, so it is useless at flying. And there are often comical crash-landings. But this doesn't matter, because it doesn't need to fly around searching for food.

Clingy chicks

Hoatzin chicks have claws on each wing, which they use to cling onto the branches around the nest. The youngsters also use their claws to climb back into the nest if they fall into the water below. The birds lose the claws after about three months.

What exactly do hoatzins eat?

82% leaves, 10% flowers and 8% fruit

SEE! NICE AND CLEAN!

BAD TASTE IN THE MOUTH

What protects this unique bird from being eaten? It turns out that this stinky bird not only smells bad – it also tastes foul! So while potential predators have no trouble catching a hoatzin, they certainly wouldn't want to eat it.

Dive to survive

When it feels threatened, a hoatzin chick performs a type of triathlon. First, it jumps out of its nest into the water below. Next, it flaps underwater to a bank further away. Finally, it emerges from the water and hauls itself up a branch using its wing claws.

WANT MORE?

Learn more ☆ www.discoverwildlife.com/animals/hoatzin-meet-stink-bird

LAW OF THE FAVELA

Perched on hillsides, shanty-towns spill down towards some of the wealthiest neighbourhoods in Rio de Janeiro, Brazil. Known as *favelas*, the settlements are illegal and are not run by the Brazilian government. They are overcrowded slums, with their own lawmakers – the criminals.

DO WHAT I SAY, OR I WILL HAVE NO MERCY!

Illegal settlement
The favelas were set up in the late 19th century by African slaves when slavery was abolished. The government refused to recognize the favelas as legal settlements, and so didn't provide them with basic services, such as roads, electricity and water.

CAUTION

Run by drug runners
From the middle of the 1980s, the favelas became centres of the illegal drug trade. The drug dealers began to stock more and more weapons so that they could protect their interests. It wasn't long before they were running the favelas as well.

Kids playing
football in
a favela

SOCIAL SERVICES

Surprisingly, the criminal gangs provide the favelas with a number of social services. They may help people to pay for funerals or buy buses for transporting children to school. They also finance projects that provide medical care, education, food and shelter to street kids. The criminals also donate money to local kids' football clubs.

School's out

There are schools in the favelas, but some parents choose to send their kids elsewhere to be educated. This is because the schools in the favelas are poor, with a shortage of teachers and crowded classrooms.

Breaking the law

With no police force or law courts, the drug gangs impose their own systems of law and order. People who break the rules are dealt with swiftly and violently, sometimes losing their lives.

Gangs control
the streets.

Samba in the shanty towns

The settlements may be rickety and run by criminals, but they are also home to thriving communities with shops, markets and schools. Music and the arts flourish too – most of the samba dance schools that perform in the Rio Carnival parade are based in favelas.

WANT
MORE?

One third of Rio's population live in its 800 favelas.

The New Year is a huge celebration in Ecuador. In the days building up to it, dolls the size of humans begin to appear on the city streets. People even drive around with dolls stuck to the front of their cars. On New Year's Eve people roam the streets to see the different dolls and party. When the clock strikes midnight, all the dolls are set alight and the sky fills with smoke and exploding rockets.

ALL DOLLED UP FOR NEW YEAR

In the firing line
The dolls, known as monigotes (doll) or Años Viejo (Old Year), represent bad things from the outgoing year. They could be people that the doll burner has fallen out with, or bad events or disappointments.

Pinning on your hopes
Notes full of hopes, disappointments and regrets are often pinned to the dolls.

Out with the old
Old clothes are stuffed with sawdust or straw to form the body of the doll. The face is decorated with a colourful mask. Some people stuff their dolls with vegetables or farmyard manure. Perhaps this explains why the dolls are left on the street and not kept indoors!

In your face!

The masks are usually made of papier-mâché and can be bought at just about any market stall. People also make their own. Sometimes masks represent famous people – politicians are a popular choice, particularly the president.

Papier-mâché mask

Penny for the guys

Anyone who is out on New Year's Eve needs a pocket full of change. Young men dress up as women and call themselves 'widows' of the old year. They dance in front of cars, asking for money to help them through the new year.

ROPE BLOCK

Children also join the fun by stringing ropes across the busiest streets. When a car approaches they pull the rope tight, dropping it only when the driver gives them a coin.

Going out with a bang

To really make the New Year's celebration explosive, the *monigotes* may contain firecrackers or fireworks. These explode as the dolls burn.

Dolls displayed on a stand for New Year's Eve

WANT MORE?

For good luck, people jump over the smouldering dolls three times at midnight.

Colombia produces about 60 per cent of the world's emeralds. The finest of these are mined near Bogotá, the country's capital. Two mines, Muzo and La Pita, account for 90 per cent of the country's emerald exports.

EMERALD CITY

Standing on ceremony
Long before the Spanish invaded the country in search of gold, native peoples mined the emeralds for their gold jewellery and ceremonial objects.

BUY ONE, GET ONE FREE!

Ancient jewellery

Stone of fire
Colombian emeralds are prized for their clearness and sparkle. The emeralds range in colour from a light yellowish-green to a deep, dark bluish-green.

TREASURE HUNTERS

Many miners plunder the mines illegally. By day, treasure hunters scour the riverbed and scavenge the mining waste for emeralds that may have been missed by the miners. At night, they tunnel into the hillsides, risking suffocation and cave-ins in their search for the stones.

Emerald dealers selling their wares on an emerald market in Bogotá.

People sifting through the waste heaps outside the mines, trying to find emeralds.

Emerald war

In the 1980s, Pablo Escobar, the head of the Medellin drug gang, tried to take over the emerald mines of Muzo. When the bosses of the emerald industry refused to hand over the mines, the area around Muzo found itself on the front line of a bloody war. Up to 3000 people died before the drug lord gave up. Escobar was executed for his crimes.

Emerald district

After they are cut and polished, most emeralds are sold in the emerald district in downtown Bogotá. The only light anyone trusts to examine an emerald is sunlight. That's why all the deals are done in the street or next to a window.

The house of Pablo Escobar, where he was killed by soldiers.

WANT MORE?

Learn more ★ www.cia.gov/library/publications/the-world-factbook/geos/co.html

LAND LOVERS

You may wonder why Bolivia has its own navy. After all, it is a landlocked country, with no access to the sea. This wasn't always the case, however. When the navy was established Bolivia did own a bit of the Pacific coastline. Then it lost it to Chile during the War of the Pacific between 1879 and 1883. Today, the navy symbolises the hope that the country will one day regain its lost territory. In the meantime, the 5000-strong force patrols Lake Titicaca and the country's many vast rivers.

I GET SEASICK ANYWAY!

The Bolivian Naval Force has about 2000 naval infantry and marines.

The 'Día del Mar is celebrated on 23 March

Day of the sea
The navy takes part in many parades and government functions. One of the most important events is the annual *Día del Mar*, or Day of the Sea. The navy marches in a parade, and the Bolivian government asks Chile officially for access to the Pacific Ocean.

Nice neighbours

Many of the naval officers do their ocean training aboard Argentinian naval ships. The force's main base is at Copacabana on Lake Titicaca. This is located on a peninsula separated from the rest of Bolivia, so to get there you have to go through Peru.

Serving its country

As well as patrolling Lake Titicaca, the Bolivian navy patrols the country's great rivers. It fights smuggling, delivers supplies to remote rural areas and rescues people and livestock during floods.

All hands on deck

In 1989 the navy helped archaeologists to search Lake Titicaca for the ruins of an ancient temple built by the people of Tiwanaku. And in 2002, they supplied the manpower to pull a 9-tonne (9.9 ton) rock onto a reed boat on the lake. The experiment was to see if the people of Tiwanaku could have used reed boats to move the rocks used to build their monoliths. The experiment was a success.

Reed boat

THE OCEAN'S THAT WAY!

La Paz's high-rise football ground

FIT FOR FIFA

In 2007, FIFA, world football's governing body, banned international games from being played at more than 2500m (8200ft) above sea level, fearing for players' health. The ban wasn't liked in Bolivia, where games at La Paz are played at 3600m (11,800ft) above sea level. Soon the Bolivian navy stepped in to help. They staged exercises on high peaks in the Andes and managed to convince FIFA its health concerns were groundless.

WANT MORE?

The Bolivian Navy has a single sea-going vessel, docked in Argentina.

The huge Christ the Redeemer statue watching over the city is probably the first thing that comes to mind when you think about Rio de Janeiro. Built between 1922 and 1931, the statue was named as one of the New Seven Wonders of the World in 2007. Rio's guardian angel could do with one itself, for it is continually under attack – sometimes from very unexpected quarters.

FATHER, FORGIVE THEM

30m
(98ft)

The statue is 30m (98ft) tall, not including its 8m (26ft) pedestal. Its arms stretch 28m (92ft) wide.

THAT WAS SOME FISH!

I THINK WE'VE BEEN SPOTTED!

Holey water
Moist, salty air coming off the sea stains the pale-green stone tiles that cover the statue. Heavy rain chisels pits in the surface of the tiles. And a combination of rain and the heat of the Sun cracks the grouting between the tiles and the concrete beneath.

Translated, one bit of graffiti said, 'When the cat's away the mice will play'.

Scandal of the vandals

While the statue was being given a facelift in 2010, it got a makeover that nobody was expecting. On 14 April, vandals climbed scaffolding to spray graffiti all over the head and shoulders. People were outraged. The lord mayor of the city called the vandalism 'a crime against the nation'. A week after the incident, the culprits turned themselves in to the police.

NOT YOU AGAIN!

An act of God

When an electrical storm hit in February 2008, it was discovered that lightning rods that were supposed to protect the statue had not been installed properly. Being the tallest structure around, the iron was the natural target. Bolts of lightning cracked off pieces of the fingertips, head and eyebrows.

In the hands of God

Using mountaineering equipment, environmental protesters scaled the statue in 2002 and 2006. They unfurled banners to make their point. The activists were arrested as soon as they abseiled to the bottom.

WANT MORE?

You need to climb 220 steps just to reach the base of the statue.

LET'S SAMBA!

Every year Rio de Janeiro erupts into Carnival. The main focus of it is the Rio Samba Parade – a hotly contested competition between the city's samba dance schools. This is a highly organised show on a grand scale. Each samba school has between 3000 and 6000 members taking part.

Non-stop carnival

As soon as a carnival is over, the samba schools begin to prepare for the next year. First, the theme is chosen. Then the school's samba song is selected, while the school's carnival designer sketches out designs for the costumes and the floats. When they are ready, the sketches move into production. About three months before the event, dancing rehearsals begin.

HELLO, MUM!

THERE SHE IS!

SAMBADROME

Until 1984 the main competition was on Avenue Presidente Vargas, one of Rio's major routes, with the rest of the carnival filling the other streets in the city. Nowadays, the parade takes place in the Sambadrome, a venue built specially for this event.

Attaching the costumes' beads and sequins is painstaking work.

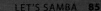

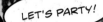

LET'S PARTY!

MAKING A SONG AND DANCE OF IT

A samba school's band is made up of 250–350 percussionists – mainly drummers. The beats of the percussion instruments give life and energy to the whole parade.

The schools' annual samba songs are recorded and released to the record shops just in time for Christmas.

JULGADORES

NREDO | SAMBA ENREDO | MESTRE SALA E PORTA BANDEIRA | BATERIA | CO DE

JUDGING CATEGORIES

PERCUSSION BAND
SAMBA SUNG
HARMONY
FLOW AND SPIRIT
THEME OF THE YEAR
OVERALL IMPRESSION
FLOATS AND PROPS
COSTUMES
VANGUARD GROUP
(group of about 12 dancers that dance ahead of their school)
FLAG-CARRYING COUPLE (two people who carry the school's flag)

School exams
The schools are judged in ten categories. There are four judges for each category, making 40 judges altogether. The judges sit in booths dotted along the route.

Keeping time
The event is so popular and there are so many samba schools competing that in 1971 organisers set a time limit for the performance of each team.

WANT MORE?

See what is planned for the next Carnival ☆ www.rio-carnival.net

PUTTING GALAPAGOS ON THE MAP

The most important visitor ever to set foot on the Galapagos Islands was the English naturalist Charles Darwin. He sailed there in 1835 on board HMS *Beagle*. On the islands, Darwin found plants, birds and reptiles that existed nowhere else on Earth. After he got back to England, Darwin came up with the theory that the animal species evolved, or changed gradually, to survive in the environments they lived in. It was one of the most important scientific theories of all time.

Beagle's about
The *Beagle* was on its way back to England after spending three years charting the coasts of South America when it arrived at the islands.

Specimens of finches collected by Darwin are kept at the Natural History Museum in London.

Charles Darwin

Finch

Survival of the finches
Darwin saw that the finches on the different islands were similar, but varied in their size, beaks and claws. For example, the shapes of the birds' beaks were different and were suited to eating whatever the birds' food source was. He decided that the birds had changed over time to suit the island environment.

Causing a stink

The first island Darwin visited was Chatham Island, known today as San Cristobal. Boy did he moan about it! According to him, the air was too muggy and the plants were smelly. He was particularly repulsed by the marine iguanas, which he'd never seen before. He described them as hideous, dirty and sluggish on land.

Shell food

No one worried about animal conservation in those days. Darwin and the *Beagle*'s crew saw the island's giant tortoises as a source of food, and assumed there was an endless supply of them. The men captured 50 tortoises to eat on the voyage home.

YOU'RE NO OIL PAINTING YOURSELF!

HMS *Beagle*

Eggstinction

Ten years after Darwin left the Galapagos, tortoises became extinct on some of the islands. They died out because of over-hunting by the crews of visiting ships, which also brought rats that ate their eggs.

UH-OH...

WANT MORE?

Learn more ☆ www.savegalapagos.org/galapagos/charles-darwin.shtml

ROAD OF DEATH

The North Yungas Road in Bolivia is by far the most dangerous road on the planet. It is so dangerous that it has earned the nickname *El Camino de la Muerte*, which is Spanish for 'road of death'. Stretching about 70km (43mi) between La Paz and Coroico, it is narrow, has ridiculously tight hairpin bends and terrifying sheer drops.

Deadly markers
Crosses marking the site of fatal accidents are dotted along the road.

On average, 26 vehicles plummet over the edge each year.

War workers
Paraguayan prisoners, captured during the Chaco War in the 1930s, built the road. It is one of the few routes that connects the Amazon rainforest region of northern Bolivia to the major city of La Paz.

Maintaining the road is costly and difficult.

HEY, IT LOOKS GOOD TO ME!

Rollercoaster road
The road certainly isn't for the faint-hearted. It goes up and down like a rollercoaster ride. And as it winds through the mountains, the landscape changes dramatically, from barren icy terrain to sub-tropical rainforest. It has no guard rails but there are sheer drops of around 800m (2625ft).

Killer conditions
Most of the road is no wider than 3.2m (10ft), and many parts are unpaved. On top of this, rain, fog and dust can make it difficult for drivers to see where they are going. In many places the road is muddy and slippery.

RULES OF DEATH ROAD
The North Yungas Road has its own rules. Unlike in the rest of Bolivia, vehicles drive on the left side. This means the driver can see the edge of the road, making passing safer.

WEEEEEE!

AND IF YOU LOOK TO YOUR LEFT... ARRRGH!

Dicing with death
Since the 1990s, the reputation of the road has spread, and the road is now a popular tourist destination, drawing about 25,000 thrillseekers a year. Mountain biking enthusiasts have made it the ultimate destination for downhill biking.

WANT MORE?

At least 18 cyclists have died falling from the road since 1998.

A QUACKING GAME

The game of *pato* has been played in Argentina since the 17th century, and has been the national sport since 1953. Pato, which means duck in Spanish, is played on horseback. Also known as horseball, it is a bit like a cross between polo and basketball. Nowadays, football is more popular than pato and most Argentinians know very little about their national sport.

THEY'RE ALL QUACKERS!

Fowl play

Pato was first played by cowboys known as *gauchos*. They originally played with a live duck, which usually died during the match. Playing fields would stretch the distance between neighbouring ranches. The first team to reach its own ranch house with the duck was the winner. The game was rough, with falls, fights and trampling hooves. Injuries and even deaths were common.

OI! GET YOUR OWN BALL.

International events, including the World Championship, are held in Argentina.

HORSEPLAY

Today pato is played on an open field between two teams of four horsemen each. The riders try to fling the ball through the opposing team's goal. A player must hold the ball with his arm outstretched so that other players have a chance of swiping it from him. The game is divided into six 8-minute sessions. At the end of these, the team with the most goals is the winner.

Grave concerns

In 1796 a Catholic priest refused to give a Christian burial to any pato player who died during a game. Throughout the 19th century, local governments banned games.

GAME ON!

Juan Perón

In 2010 a government senator tried but failed to introduce a law replacing pato with soccer as the national sport of Argentina.

Making it official

In the 1930s pato was permitted once more when ranch owner Alberto del Castillo set out strict rules of play. The duck was replaced with a leather ball and the game became respectable. In 1953, President Juan Perón declared pato Argentina's national game.

70,000 spectators

4000 spectators

National sport or lame duck?

Pato has become less popular as Argentina has become more urban and as owning a horse has become a luxury. Only about 4000 spectators turn up to see big pato games in Buenos Aires, whereas 70,000 turn out for big-team soccer games in the city.

WANT MORE?

For more info about the national sport of Argentina ✯ www.vamospanish.com

ANT EATERS

Colombian people have been snacking on leafcutter ants for centuries. The ones they eat, *Atta laevigata*, are the largest species of leafcutter ant in the world. They are packed with protein and taste a little like crispy bacon.

DOES MY BUM LOOK BIG IN THIS?

Big bummed ants
The ants are more commonly known as *Hormiga culona*, which roughly translates as large-bottomed ant. And boy do they have big bums!

A bigger bite
People collecting the ants often get wounded by the creatures, which use their huge jaws to bite their captors.

Female ant full of eggs

Protein packed
Only the female ants are eaten. They are harvested between March and June during the mating season when they are full of protein because they are bloated with eggs.

25mm
(0.9in)
The length of the average *Atta laevigata*

OFF WITH HER HEAD!

To prepare the ant for the pot, the cook pinches the middle section of the body tightly and then pulls off the head. The legs and wings are next. The bodies are soaked in salty water overnight.

DO YOU THINK HE SAW ME?

Ready to roast
The ants are toasted in pans. There is no need for oil as it is released from the insects as they cook.

ANTS CROSSING

FUNGUS FARMERS

When they are not being eaten themselves, the ants grow their own food by cutting down leaves and using them to grow a fungus which they eat.

WANT MORE?

Toasted leafcutter ants are exported to Canada, Japan and England.

INDEX

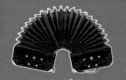

NOT-FOR-PARENTS
SOUTH AMERICA
EVERYTHING YOU EVER WANTED TO KNOW

1st Edition
Published September 2013

WELDONOWEN

Conceived by Weldon Owen in partnership with Lonely Planet
Produced by Weldon Owen Limited
An imprint of Red Lemon Press Limited
Northburgh House,
10 Northburgh Street
London, EC1V 0AT, UK
© 2013 Weldon Owen Limited

Project managed and commissioned by Dynamo Ltd
Project manager Alison Gadsby
Project editor Gaby Goldsack-Simmonds
Designer Richard Jewitt
Picture researcher Sarah Ross
Indexer Marie Lorimer

Published by
Lonely Planet Publications Pty Ltd ABN 36 005 607 983
90 Maribyrnong St, Footscray, Victoria 3011, Australia

ISBN 978-1-74321-915-7

Printed and bound in China by 1010 Printing Int Ltd
9 8 7 6 5 4 3 2 1

All rights reserved. No part of this publication may be reproduced, stored
in a retrieval system or transmitted in any form or by any means, electronic,
mechanical, photocopying, recording or otherwise, except brief extracts
for the purpose of review, without the written permission of the publisher.

Lonely Planet and the Lonely Planet logo are trademarks of Lonely Planet
and are registered in the US Patent and Trademark Office and in other
countries. Lonely Planet does not allow its name or logo to be
appropriated by commercial establishments, such as retailers, restaurants
or hotels. Please let us know of any misuses: www.lonelyplanet.com/ip.

Disclaimer
Although Weldon Owen Limited and Lonely Planet have taken all
reasonable care in gathering information for this title, we make no
warranty about its accuracy or completeness or, to the maximum
extent permitted, disclaim all liability. Wherever possible, we will
endeavour to correct any errors of fact at reprint.

www.redlemonpress.com

Red Lemon Press Limited is part of
the Bonnier Publishing Group
www.bonnierpublishing.com

Credits and acknowledegments

KEY – tl top left, tc top centre, tr top right, cl centre left, c centre,
cr centre right, bl bottom left, bc bottom centre, br bottom right.

All images © Shutterstock except:

8cl, 9tl, 9br, 16bl, 17cr, 17bl, 19bl, 19br, 26bl, 27br, 30tl, 31tl, 31bl, 38tr,
40tr, 44cl, 45tl, 45tr, 46tr, 46br, 47tr, 47cl, 49tr, 58tr, 59tr, 59br, 62tr, 76cr,
76br, 76tr, 76c, 77tr, 77cr, 81cr, 85tr, 88c, 92cl, 93c **Alamy**; 2bc, 2bl, 3tl,
10bl, 11cl, 19tc, 19bc, 21tr, 22cl, 24cl, 25bl, 28tr, 28cr, 29bl, 32cr, 35tr,
36cl, 37bl, 44br, 48br, 51bl, 52tr, 52cl, 52bc, 52br, 53tr, 53bl, 54bl, 55cl,
61cr, 62cr, 63tr, 65tr, 65cl, 65br, 67cr, 68cl, 68cr, 68bl, 69tr, 69bl, 70c,
71tl, 72bl, 73bl, 75tl, 75cr, 75bl, 76br, 77tc, 80tr, 80b, 85c, 91tr **Corbis**;
6cr, 8tr, 11tr, 11br, 13tr, 13br, 15bl, 16tr, 23tr, 23cl, 34tr, 36bl, 37cr, 43bl,
48cl, 50tr, 50br, 54tr, 55br, 56cr, 61br, 75br, 76cr, 83tl, 83bl, 85tl, 86c,
88bl, 89tr, 93bl **Getty Images**; 42tr, 43c, 77br, 83cr **Rex Features**;
39br **Eyevine**.

Cover illustrations by **Chris Corr**

All illustrations and maps copyright 2013 Weldon Owen Limited

LONELY PLANET OFFICES

Australia Head Office
Locked Bag 1, Footscray, Victoria 3011
Phone 03 8379 8000   Fax 03 8379 8111

USA
150 Linden St, Oakland, CA 94607
Phone 510 250 6400   Toll free 800 275 8555   Fax 510 893 8572

UK
Media Centre, 201 Wood Lane, London W12 7TQ
Phone 020 8433 1333   Fax 020 8702 0112

lonelyplanet.com/contact

MIX
Paper from
responsible sources
FSC™ C021741

Paper in this book is certified against
the Forest Stewardship Council™
standards. FSC™ promotes
environmentally responsible, socially
beneficial and economically viable
management of the world's forests.